SUNRISE IN AFRICA

By

Benedicta Mbanuzue

www.BeneNaomiPoems.com

New Millennium
192 Kennington Road, London SE11 4LD

Set in 11pt Times New Roman type-face.
Printed and bound by Arm Crown Ltd. Uxbridge Road, Middx.
Issued by New Millennium.*
*An imprint of The Professional Authors' & Publishers' Association (PAPA).

Acknowledgements

To, my husband, Felix
and my son, Kingsley. Your limitless patience
and support inspired me to turn my dream into reality.

My special thanks also to:
Andrew Ekwuru, Godson Echebima
and Gold Ndukwe for their support.

Contents

SUNRISE IN AFRICA

As the day began to dawn
Up on the trees the birds were singing
Night crickets, their music no longer heard
Palm leaves whispering as the gentle breeze glided across.

Peeping through my window
On the horizon the sun was rising behind the palms
An unforgettable sight
Nature displayed her beauty.

Speechless with my arms folded
My eyes gazing, mouth wide open
How lovely, how wonderful
Breathtaking, I watched in amazement.

Colours beyond my imagination
Never have I seen anything so beautiful
I was lost in my thoughts
Feeling as if my soul has left my body.

Gracefully coming through the clouds, the sun appeared
Majestically, radiating like a king in a robe of colours
Being ushered to sit on his throne
Wonderful, wonderful, my lips muttered.

Can't remember how long my eyes remained unblinked
Or how long was the motionlessness of my entire body
But of one thing I was certain
Nature had put me in a trance.

Slowly his rays began to spread
Like the sea spreading her waves
The unimaginable colours began to disappear
Too strong, my eyes were too weak to focus.

As he emerged fully
Leaving the sky immaculately white
I was glad to be part of this wonderful universe, I said
As I left, taking with me this lasting scenery.

THE OLD MAN AND HIS FLUTE

The old man's house next to the stream
Thatched roof, red mud walls
To enter, you've got to crawl
Its cool, to absorb the tropical heat
While the old man played his flute.

Howling noises made by the stream
As it rustles through the stones
Adding more melody to the ears
Fishes become the dancers
While the old man played his flute.

Bridge built with bamboo trees
Swinging from side to side
Be careful walking on it
Could break when not looking
While the old man played his flute.

Palm trees and bamboo trees
Form the shade around the stream
At night the moon peeps through
To say goodnight with a beam of light
While the old man played his flute.

Misty and hazy early morning
Dew drops on green grass below
Sparkling like scattered diamonds
Birds hovering between the trees
While the old man played his flute.

NDIDI MY LOVE

Tomorrow you'll be leaving to a far away country
Thousands of miles from home
The loss of you will break my heart
Ndidi my love, let nobody change your mind.

Although we'll be far apart
I will still remember
All the promises we've made
Ndidi my love, let nobody change your mind.

Remember the coconut tree
Under which we sat and dreamt
The moon was full, crickets played their music
Ndidi my love, let nobody change your mind.

As the stars above are uncountable
So is my love for you
When I am grey and sixty, I'll still be waiting
Ndidi my love, let nobody change your mind.

You'll write weekly as you promised
If you stop writing, I'll stop living
Life for me without you will be worthless here
Ndidi my love, let nobody change your mind.

No harm will come to you, I pray
Until in my arms I hold you once again
Your head on my shoulder to rest
Ndidi my love, let nobody change your mind.

BABY

Close to my heart
I hold you so dear
Cry not my love
Mother will not go away.

Cuddled in my arms
Where you belonged
Here you look for shelter
Mother will not go away.

Hold tight tiny hands
Little feet stand firm
Nothing to fear, all is well
Mother will not go away.

Baby face full of smiles
The day for me you brightened
In joy as well as sorrow
Mother will not go away.

Unconditional is mother's love
The memories of your birth
More than precious stone to me
Mother will not go away.

Lullabies sung while baby sleeps
Sweet dreams my loved one
When you wake I'll be here
Mother will not go away.

MY CHILD

I loved you before you were born
Your movement in my womb brought tears of joy to my eyes
I saw your face in my dreams even before your conception
Having you gave a new meaning to my life.

Although you put me out of shape
Made me eat things not to my taste
I moaned and groaned with discomfort
Having you gave a new meaning to my life.

Your cries were music to my ears
Your smile brightened my day
Your first word "Mama" brought joy to my heart
Having you gave a new meaning to my life.

Over the years I've watched you grow
I shared your joys and sorrows
Loved and absorbed all your mischief
Having you gave a new meaning to my life.

Science has done wonders, I agree
But a child conceived and born
Is the greatest miracle ever seen
Having you gave a new meaning to my life.

LEAVING HOME

Sad to leave the house where I was born
Although Mama knew I left a long time ago
The folks I knew are no longer here
Stranger I have become amongst my people
No longer at ease with myself
If I leave I stand a better chance
Of achieving the goal I set for myself
Although unsure and afraid of the unknown
These are chances I've got to take
For I will always try something once
These are things I've got to do alone
Sad to leave the house where I was born
But Mama knew I left long time ago.

TOMORROW

As I walked home late evening
To drown my sorrows with palm wine
My heart near to breaking point
Tomorrow my love will be gone
To far away country
Unable to control my tears, I said
Who will be there to cook your meals?
Who will darn your socks and mend your clothes?
Who will shine your shoes?
Who will listen and hear what you say?
Whose shoulder will you cry on?
Most importantly, who will love you as I do?
Tomorrow, I wish you would never come.

6

THE WARRIOR

He will be there tomorrow
His heart fast-beating
Coming to manhood, he must be
Initiated, or he will not belong.

Lying on palm leaves, skin bare
Painted with red and white chalk
Bowl of kola and palm kernel nuts
Placed at the feet of the young warrior.

Surrounded by men already initiated
The sound of drums call his name
Women warned not to be seen
The day is only for the warriors.

Whipped at the heat of the sun
Not a sigh is heaved
This is the rule of our ancestors
It is the day of the warriors.

At last he is one of them
Celebration and jubilation
Wait until the moon comes out
The warrior will choose a bride.

THE NEW YAM FESTIVAL

This was the expected day
Ugoma the dancer was excited
At the first cock crow
Children were chanting going to the spring.

Walking the narrow pathway
Smaller ones in front, big ones behind
Making sure they were protected
This was how things used to be.

Akara and Akamu for their breakfast
Time for them to fetch fire wood too
Soon mothers' cooking
Will be smelt everywhere.

She was the head dancer
Hair in plaits, skin decorated in dyes
Bead of colours around her waist and ankles
The Chief's guests to be entertained.

Boys with colourful uniforms beat the drums
The ceremony about to start
She did her majestic walk
This was like a starter before the main course.

Now she danced, leaped into the air, danced on
Every body movement is hailed
Every dancing step excited the crowd
Money is showered on her
In admiration of her performance.

MY MOTHER

As a baby I lay in my cradle
Mother peeped in and gave a smile
She put her finger in my hand
And I held tight to feel assured
I am here to protect you
With a smile I responded,
Yes mother, I am safe in your hands.

When I began to sit
She was always there to assure me
That when I fall forwards or backwards,
Towards my right or my left
Nothing would hurt you, I'm here to protect you
With a smile I responded,
Yes mother, I am safe in your hands.

When I began to stand
She'd always put her hands around me
To ensure I was safe if I fell
She'd always be ready to catch me
Don't be afraid I'm here to protect you
With a smile, I responded,
Yes mother, I am safe in your hands.

When I took my first step
I could see some tears of joy in her eyes
She was speechless and humbled herself
She put her hands out and I held tight
Don't be afraid, I'm here to protect you
With a smile I responded,
Yes mother, I am safe in your hands.

Mother worried about my well-being
Eating, sleeping, walking or playing
She watched me
Cheerful, morose or sad
She offered her hands and I grabbed them
Mothers are supreme.

NATURE UNDISTURBED

Here is the land of my choice
Where nature has never been disturbed
Her beauty from the start never changing
The land I longed so much to see.

The smell of wild flowers fill the air
Perfumed with the most precious oil
The stream gently flowing down the valley
Fishes never in a hurry to swim
No threats to their lives can they observe.

The birds of the air full of joy
Provide twenty-four hour melody
Naturally they sing, never in competition
No fear, no pressure of losing.

Sandy beaches along the shores
Glitter like diamonds and pearls
As the sun's rays fall on the river banks
This is the land where nature has retained
Its original present and past beauties.

The trees looked elegant, tall and slim
As the wind blew from all directions
They seemed to be doing a swan dance
Although they looked as if they were about to break
Watching them hypnotise me.

Here the grass is green all year round
Sea breezes gently touching the body
Makes me feel sleepy all day long
I tend to forget there is another world out there
What need have I got to rush?

SURVIVAL

Lying low waiting for his prey
Dry season over stayed her time
Survival is the name of the game
The king of the forest lies in wait.

Rising dust in mid-air
His heart leapt with joy
Aiming not to miss
The king of the forest lies in wait.

Soon this way they must pass
In search of water to drink
A herd of antelopes approaching
The king of the forest lies in wait.

Swiftly he pounced on her
She was the last to follow the pack
Piercing his teeth through the neck
This is how the king operates.

From where he stood
It was kill or be killed
This could be the last meal
Till tomorrow, who knows?

THE COCK CROWS

Ko koro ro koo!
The cock has become confused
The moon was late at night
Can we always depend on others?

The village chief sounded the gong
Palm wine tapper up on the tree
The old man smoking his pipe
Can we always depend on others?

Children with pots on their heads
Chanting as they walked to the stream
The village life is all in chaos
Can we always depend on others?

Mothers with babies on their backs
Sweeping the yard ready for the farm
Yet no sign of day break
Can we always depend on others?

The moon continued to shine
No sign of the sun in sight
Quickly they all returned
To their bamboo beds and mosquito nets.

The village time-keeper deceived by nature
Who in turn deceived man
Together they all agreed
It was going to be a long day
Can we always depend on others?

GOING HOME

Going home, going home
How good it is to be going home
Home of tradition, culture and custom
Too long since I was here.

Some of the infants I had known
Heads of their families they have become
Others have gone to towns and cities
Too long since I was here.

Some mates of mine no longer here
Those present, how old they looked
I too, must look the same
Too long since I was here.

The coconut and mango trees
The moon dance, the village square
Nothing looks the same anymore
Too long since I was here.

The village Church
Where once I worshipped as a child
Like a stranger I asked many questions
Too long since I was here.

Evening was fast approaching
Confused and frustrated I went to my bed
Seeking calm and understanding
Tomorrow is another day of discovery.

REFLECTION

Standing here by the old crumbled house
I reflected on how things used to be
How could I have forgotten them, I asked
This was the house where I grew up
This was the place where I had been very very happy.

Often, this place for granted I took
Always looking at another man's green grass
Forgetting that mine was even greener
This was the house where I grew up
This was the place where I had been very very happy.

Grumbling about home as I often did
Mother often yelling and welling at me
Tormented by my little brother Uche
This was the house where I grew up
This was the place where I had been very very happy.

Here is where I am most loved, my childhood memories stored
Some of which I love to remember, others to forget
Yet so much they all meant to me
This was the house where I grew up
This was the place where I had been very very happy.

Mother's shoulders were always there for me
She criticised without malice
Genuineness was her way of life
This was the house where I grew up
This was the place where I had been very very happy.

Home sweet home, her love unconditional
Where confidentiality remained in a safe
There will never be another place like you
This was the house where I grew up
This was the place where I had been very very happy.

GRIEF

So bright and beautiful
Egbichi was a friend I'll never forget
She was full of love and laughter
We played and danced in the moonlight
Quarrels were quickly settled
You never saw one without the other
Often we were called 'the twins'
She was eight and I was nine
When she was called to heaven

Years have passed by
Yet like yesterday it seems
They say that time heals every wound
But this is one wound time has forgotten to heal
Never has a day passed, my dear
Without me remembering you
How I wished I could wind the clock back
Your smiles and laughter
Everything beautiful reminds me of you
I miss you. Oh! how very much I do.

LAUGHTER

Laughter is like the seven-lobe kola-nut
A thing we do not get often
Can you tell me my friend
When last did you have a good laugh?

A laughing face glows in the midst of gloom
The blood tickles the heart, the body relaxes
Burden recedes before laughter
When last did you have a good laugh?

Life's journey is short
Summons to creator sudden
Why then not stop and ask
When last did you have a good laugh?

Laughter is scarce
But a satisfying experience
Why then not have more of it?
And, thank heavens for a good laugh.

THE ONES WE LOVE MOST

Sometimes we tend to forget
That although they have grown in age and size
Deep down there remains a hollow inside
Which needs to be filled with love.

Life demands so much from us
Trying to put our houses in order
Running up and down until dusk
Sometimes we hardly have time to say Hello!

Days run into weeks, weeks into months
Before we know it, it will be the new millennium
What have we done all these years ?
That we had no time to give a little hug.

Could we remember when last
We took a trip to get away from it all
To be able to tell each other how you feel
To listen and hear actually what was said.

Have a good laugh from the heart
Hug each other, say I love you, and mean it
Everyone needs this from time to time
This is the greatest tonic of life.

THE FIRST SPEECH

Sleepless night he'd had
Today he would make
His first speech to his people
By morning he was a wreck.

Up early ready before the time
Very little breakfast, appetite gone
Voice like one with a frog in his throat
Bags under the eyes, yes, a wreck he was.

Time was up, he had to go
As he stood on the platform
Uncountable was his heartbeat
He could do with dibia somebody said.

Sweat dripping from his hands
Teeth clattering, knees weak
Mouth dried like the harmattan wind
They all looked at him with their mouths open.

He straightened his jacket
Cleared his throat of nothing
Gasping for breath as if he had run a mile
He peered through the crowd with his heavy glasses.

Well he started, hope your journey here was smooth
Yes, yes, yes they replied and clapped
He had broken the ice
From then on he never looked back.

MY FATHER

As a child
I watched my father come and go
He was like a giant and I was like a mouse
His footsteps shook the ground
But when he held me in his arms
I felt his gentleness all over me
Little did I know that father is human.

He often speaks to me in a loud voice
Could he be angry?
But when I look into his eyes
I could see that father was afraid
Afraid of what?
Afraid that I might fail him, I suspected
Then I realise that father is human.

I am afraid when father speaks
Afraid when he is silent
What could he be thinking I ask myself
Have I always made him angry I wonder
I never realised that father was amazed
Amazed how much I have grown
Little did I know that father is human.

Walking along the street one day
I summoned up courage to ask my father
Have I always made you angry?
But to my greatest surprise
He told me that I was the best thing that ever happened to him
And I'll understand when I have a child of my own
Little did I know that father is human.

Father has always been my idol
His strength, perseverance and courage
To me he can never do any wrong
Yet he often seeks my advise
One day I will know what makes him tick
For me he is the greatest Dad of all
Little did I know that father is human.

BEAUTIFUL AFRICA

AFRICA! AFRICA! what are you to me?
The colonised giant of Africa
The land of the rising sun
The land of long and short shadows.

Full moon on a clear blue sky littered with myriad stars
The land of dry and rainy seasons and waterfalls
The evergreen forest, swampy land colonised by mosquitoes
The land of palm and coconut trees.

Wild flowers fill the air with their perfume
Wildlife flourishes in abundance
The sound of cricket and frog croaks fill the night
Where the cock crows to tell the time.

The land of superstitions, rituals and customs
The land of tribal and inter-tribal wars
Where the ancestors are constantly consulted
Where men are initiated or else do not belong.

The land of distant drums and talking gongs
Children comfortably carried on their mother's back
Girls with hair plaited, wearing ankle beads of many colours
The land of family bonds and extended family ties.

Where childhood memories are endeared
Nicknamed 'The Dark Continent'
The ever changing Africa
AFRICA! AFRICA! you are everything to me.

CHILDHOOD MEMORIES

Lonely, through the memories of my childhood, I wondered
The children I used to know, we were friends
Under the coconut trees, we played when the moon was full
By our shadows and the cock crow, we could tell the time.

Every family knew every child by their names
We went in groups to fetch firewood and water
Carrying the earthenware pots on our heads
Often they were broken before we got home.

Every house provided us with shelter
Mothers did not worry where their children were
Sharing was the order of the day
Mosquitos were our greatest enemy.

Children walked the streets without fear
When night fell, we listened to our grandfathers
Telling us stories of our ancestors
And how they fought the tribal wars.

School days, when we were whipped
For the slightest disobedience
Parents were always on the teacher's side
You obey, dare not complain.

Our mud-walled, thatched roof house
Surrounded with wild flowers, that perfumed the air
Both young and old were welcomed
No guest left our house on an empty stomach.

Traditions, customs, superstitions and rituals rule the land
We looked forward to Xmas and New Yam festivals
Life was good, each cared for the other
But even as children, the boys had more latitude.

There, I stood along the pathway
Amongst the ruins of crumbling houses and fallen trees
Where life once blossomed in abundance
Darkness was approaching, no bush lamps burned.

Those years have gone too quickly
My mates have scattered far and wide
Some dead, others wandered in search of gold
Never to their homes would they return.

As the sun sets the sound of crickets could be heard everywhere
Reflecting on how things used to be
Tears ran down my cheeks
Yesterday has gone, like my folks, I'd better be moving on.

REASSURANCE

Night has become an unwelcome guest.
It has been a long day.
Nothing seemed to be going right.
My best friend has fallen ill.
Medications were to no avail.
Signs of recovery seem remote.
My anxiety turned to confusion.
Hospital admission becomes inevitable.
Time has become too precious.
Nurses were rushing here and there.
Not one word was said to me,
Although each was doing her duty, I agreed.
But only one nurse got my praise,
The nurse who reassured and put my mind at ease.

FAMILY

Family, that part of one's world
Which is cherished and enclosed like a cocoon
Difficult to penetrate
You might be let into half of their secret
The other half remains undisclosed.

Family is like a tree with her tap-root
Buried deep into the soil
Family is like a colony of ants
You touch one, you touch all
You are fought with every weapon at hand.

Family is like a house
Only the owner knows her contents
As an outsider you might know just a few
Things tucked into the closet remain their secret
They alone know when, how, and where it hurts.

No two families are alike
Each has her own ways of coping
With the ups and downs of life
Needing a little help from their friends
From those with their interests at heart.

Rich or poor, they are kings in their own right
It is difficult to know what makes them tick
Somehow this is beyond our understanding
We can only be there for them in times of need
Family is what makes us what we are.

THIS EARTHLY BODY OF MINE

Let me look after her while I can
Because when I take my last breath
No one will ever know
The way I have always looked after her
This earthly body of mine.

For those who will be there on time
To see my eyes and lips closed
Strengthen the body limbs and all
Trying not to make me look out of order
This earthly body of mine.

Do not create a new face for me
Just let me look the way I am
For I was never created beautiful
It is what is inside that matters
This earthly body of mine.

There comes another worry
What shall we put on her
There are so many to choose from
Please use only what I have chosen
For this earthly body of mine.

A well polished coffin I beg to have
Crucifix placed on top
It will delight me
The handles made of yellow metal
For this earthly body of mine.

The hymns I have already chosen
You can still sing your favourites ones
Please do sing these ones of mine
It is the best way to say good-bye
To this earthly body of mine.

To my loved ones, I say
Let your mourning be short
Who else knows your loss better than you?
So why prolong the agony
For this earthly body of mine.

Speeches must be brief and to the point
People get bored if these are prolonged
No matter how happy or sad the occasion
They want to get things over and done with
For this earthly body of mine.

THE UDARA TREE

In front of my papa's house stood a gigantic udara tree
When the moon is full, the children will come out to play
Boys with their drums, girls with ankle beads, dancing to the rhythm
O, how I wish I was an udara tree
So popular with the children and the moon
How I love to watch their smiling faces
As they dance around the udara tree.

TOMBSTONE

The old house was deserted
Walls have crumbled only a few standing
Thatched roof has since disappeared
Walking through the ruins, his mind was full of thoughts
This was where he grew up, but left years ago
His eyes kept searching for something
Suddenly he pointed, "there," he said
Hidden by overgrown grass stood a tombstone
He knelt down, bowed his head, with eyes full of tears
He said "here lies a great man, my father."

THE MAN IN MY LIFE

A pillar to lean on, I'll stand by him
One heart is all he has
Now near to a breaking point
Like a mother in my arms he lies.

I'll stand by him when he makes mistakes
I'll do the same when he gets it right
Full of pride, he will not say where it hurts
Will not cry to let out tears.

I'll cry for him to relieve his pain
No one else understands him but me
When the sun rises, I'll stand by him
At sunset, I'll stand by him too.

I can make him laugh
To lift the cloud above his head
Heavy load made lighter by my love
And gentle words to soothe his pains.

He is human. I'll try to understand
For I too could do no better
As long as I live
I'll stand by him, no matter what.

MOTHER BELOVED

Mother, sweet mother
Grief and darkness have filled my days
The vacuum and emptiness of my life
Without you, I feel helpless.

Nothing here lasts forever I know
I'm holding on to what has been
Following every step we took together
Memories are all I have.

At the mention of your name
My heart is pierced, bleeding internally
Tears never stopped to flow
Laughter has become scarce for me.

Could you not have stayed a little longer
For the one you so dearly loved
A good listener, a pillar to rest on
A bridge to cross the troubled water.

Your immeasurable love my secret keeper
To mention but a few
I alone could count my losses
No one else will ever take your place.

Not to grieve mother, is not to have loved
It is the price we pay for love
I need time to cry and time to think
Never has there been an easy way to say goodbye.

FALLING IN LOVE

I remembered the first time we met
What it was that attracted us both
The looks in your eyes and mine
The unspoken words understood by both of us alone
Falling in love is easy to do
Staying in love could be difficult.

When we used to talk to each other
Beaming with smiles enough to light the world
We could not wait to come home
That was where our hearts belonged
Falling in love is easy to do
Staying in love could be difficult.

How sure we were of each other
At first when we fell in love
When love dies, everything dies with it
The thought of coming home became a nightmare
Falling in love is easy to do.
Staying in love could be difficult.

How we used to hold hands as we walked
Now we walk a mile apart
Meal times used to be like Xmas dinner
Somehow it became the meal from hell
Falling in love is easy to do
Staying in love could be difficult.

When we looked forward for the night to come
To settle the kids and have time to ourselves
Now our discussions are shouting and yelling matches
At the end of which nothing was achieved
Falling in love is easy to do
Staying in love could be difficult.

If the cost of living goes up
We have always found a way to cope
When the cost of love goes down
There could be a way of bringing it up
Falling in love is easy to do
Staying in love could be difficult.

Now we remembered the yester-years
Recapping on how the early days used to be
Found there is more going for us than against us
Making time to say "I love you" and mean it
We still have time to make love last
To help us fall in love and stay in love.

MY PATH

My path could be rough or smooth
Short or long, none can predict
Not even I have any idea
This is the fear of the unknown
Depending on my speed
One day I hope to get there.

THE OLD COUPLE NEXT DOOR

The old couple next door
They seem to be inseparable
For you never saw one without the other
Sometimes when the weather was good
You could see them sitting in their back garden
Holding each other's hand.

I often wondered how much they meant to each other
How beautiful they must have looked in their youth
For even now in their eighties
Age does not seem to have taken anything from them
For as they hold each other's hand.
Love seems to have kept them together.

You could see the old man
Gazing into the old lady's eyes
For, years ago, she had a stroke
That left her without speech
But beyond the unspoken words
He could understand every movement she made.

Once in a while, I popped my head
To say, "Hello" and "How do you do,"
The old man would always say
"We are all right, thank you,"
I wonder if they will ever know
How much I admired them
For never have I seen a couple so much in love.

One day the old man said to me
"We are going away to be cared for,"
There was sadness in his eyes
But with a little smile, he said
"We have loved living here
And we have enjoyed knowing you."
With these words he closed his door.

Now when I look through the garden
I wonder what has become of them
No light could be seen at the windows
No welcome at the door
The garden full of weeds
Because, the old couple next door
No longer live there.

A NURSE'S PRAYER

Papa, grant me your love, patience and kindness
Required to look after the sick
Regardless of who they are, race, colour or creed
Let me treat them with respect.

Age is no barrier to good nursing care
To give by night, same care as by day.
Help me to see you in everyone
Neither their riches nor poverty to influence me.

Guide my tongue when I speak
My hands when I give my care
All for my patient's benefit
To comfort the dying and maintain their dignity.

Through me your unfailing love they'll see
For today is theirs
And tomorrow could be mine
Whatever I do, let it be for the glory of Thy name.

Amen

TRAIN JOURNEY

She stood there petrified
Unconsciously staring at the grey steel lines
Soon the beast was approaching
For her it was a nightmare
Could she cope if it stopped half-way?
Suffocation with no oxygen
How do the rest feel? she sighed
Could not read another's mind
If she could only predict the fear of the unknown
The beast could crash without warning
Dangerous to be a coward, she thought
The beast approached, the ground vibrated
She was gripped with certain fear
Her heart in her hands, as she entered
Huffing and puffing, the beast pulled off
Her body trembled, stomach turned
Cold, clammy skin, mouth dry
Her eyes shut, hands tight on the seat
Resigned now at the mercy of the beast
As the beast approached her destination
Her fears began to ease
At last all is well
After all, she thought, the beast was not that bad.

MOSQUITOES

The tropical rain has ceased to fall
Gentle wind blowing through the tree
The smell of hot sand filled the air
Water racing through the land to join the rivers
Thinking as I walked through the narrow bush path.

Ditches and puddles everywhere
Soon to be colonised by mosquito eggs
As they hatch, vampires they'll become
To suck our blood, transmitting malarial parasites
Dangerous to health, could even kill.

Little monsters, give us no peace
Sleepless nights, as they give their humming tune
They bite and run, while we hit and hurt ourselves
How little they knew that we need no music of theirs
African high-life with drums is just enough.

Whitemen did their best to see their end
Mosquito nets, often advised, educating all concerned
Medicines to prevent and cure malaria
All these did help at first
Little monsters, were too clever for man.

Team work should be our motto
From the youngest man to the oldest
Everyman to do his duty
Destroying all that give mosquitoes shelter
Hoping that at last the tyrant can be defeated.

SLEEP

Fight not, she'll always win
Takes you when you least expect
The choice is not yours to make
You'd follow where she leads.

Watch the signs, she reads your mind
Yawning, restless, with heavy eyes
Why do you have to be forced
Fight not, she'll always win.

The body grows weak
The mind hallucinates
Gradually like anaesthetic
To body and mind, peace is restored.

No clock to watch, your task is over
All comes to a stand still
You are no longer in control
Because you're no longer here.

Flying with wings of angels
Living in a world of the unknown
The impossible made possible
In our world of sleep and dream.

BEING IN LOVE

When you are in love, really in love
The sun never seems to set
Rain drops fall like glittering diamonds
Under your feet, the ground feels like a cushion
You see beauty everywhere
Like sunrays, your face radiates
In the dark it glows
Too excited, your heart beats faster
Sleep becomes a waste of time
Night is too long, day too short
Often, friends think you are drunk
They could be right, this is intoxicating
A lot could happen when you're in love
Nothing matters when you're in love
When you're in love, oh, really in love.

GRIEF II

Could there be any hope of meeting again?
Ada and Obi in love in their teens
Tragedy struck, Ada's hope shattered
Please write to mend my broken heart.

Sitting here under the mango tree
Watching the world go by
I could think of nothing but you
Please write to mend my broken heart.

Our promises signed and sealed
Not one have I broken
At thirty I'm still waiting and hoping
Please write to mend my broken heart.

Life here has become a prison
Chained to the rails, unable to escape
You alone can set me free
Please write to mend my broken heart.

They say, out of sight out of mind
This to me is quite untrue
A day has not passed without you remembered
Please write to mend my broken heart.

In my dreams I found a shooting star
Which promised to lead you home
Look out for her each night, she has my message
She will surely bring you back to me.

THE RAIN MAKER

From thatched roof hut
Stepped out feather-hatted man
Pot belly, beads around his ankles
On a bamboo chair he sat.

The talking gong announced the chief's death
The ruthless, the greedy, the pompous chief
It is witchcraft, he died in his sleep
Evil, evil, someone has done him evil.

Who can tell the truth?
If it rains, its a bad omen
Pot belly man spat on the ground
Viciously as he chewed his tobacco.

Firewood, green leaves he collected
Spiders, snails and frog legs placed on the stone
Boastfully he began to evoke rain
Disaster if it rains at funeral.

Smoke, smoke rise in the air
Bring the rain down with you
Flood the rivers, flood the roads
Our ancestors do your job.

Soon rain started to fall
Chief's funeral a poor attendance received
The rain maker announced to the people
That at last, justice had been done.

HIS MASTER'S VOICE

Oh the darkest night
Restless and lying awake
Hoping for daybreak
Nature took pity on him.

This state of unconsciousness appreciated
Here strains and stress end
The impossible becomes possible
To nature the body surrendered.

Suddenly like thunder his name was called
Interrupting this wonderful state of mind
As the voice became louder and louder
He knew he must obey.

Again and again his name was called
Where are you Lord? he asked
To him, the dream world was over
Where are you Lord, he asked.

As the voice became clearer
Speak Lord, he said
Speak for your servant is here
Ready to obey your command.

Unclean as I might be, he said
But if you need somebody
Here I am ready to go
Send me Lord, send me.

Now he knew the task will not be easy
Yet with all his heart he accepted
No regrets had he
For obeying his master's voice.

THE SAILORS

Rough from the start as they sailed
Their mast torn off before their eyes
Hitting the rock, the ship was wrecked
Leaving the men scrambling to safety.

Ruthlessly the sea continued to roar
Waves of terror spreading from side to side
Bringing with it the drowning men
Clutching at everything they saw.

Tossed up in the air the waves continued
Men swimming endlessly
The captain shouted, don't give up
Sound of his voice spread like waves.

Tropical island hidden in the West
Coconut trees dancing in the wind
White lilies spraying their perfume
The sound of crickets announcing the night.

Land at last in sight they shouted
The sound of drums echoed in the air
Natives with lights waiting to greet their guests
Dancing girls with ankle beads.

One by one they came ashore
None of them was left behind
Weary and tired on their knees they went
Kissing the ground for safety sake.

LOST LOVE

So many years I've loved you
Nobody, nobody ever knew
How much I have cared
Within me the battle went on
Darling,' I've loved you for so many years.

This morning I meant to call
Can't keep it secret any more
With shaking hands I dialled the number
No longer here, the voice said
Darling, I've loved you for so many years.

I kept hoping and praying
Again, trembling, the number I dialled
No longer here, repeated the voice
My fault, my fault, I cried
Darling, I've loved you for so many years.

My lost love how can I tell you
That all these years I've loved you
Don't know if you did notice
Should have told you earlier than this
Darling, I've loved you for so many years.

Night after night I lay awake
My pillows soaked with tears
Knowing you're in another's arms
No one will ever take your place
Darling, I've loved you for so many years.

AGEING

Nkechi, by her window stood
Watching the leaves of the iroko tree
Turned brown and dry
Falling as the wind blows
This is harmattan season
One by one the leaves fell
Until not a leaf was left on the tree
Stripped of her beauty and pride
She stood bare and unattractive
The leaves will bloom when the rainy season comes
She looked in the mirror and said
One day my hair will turn grey and thin
Like the leaves they will fall
Until no hair is left on my head
But unlike the iroko tree, she said
The rainy season will make no difference.

OGBUAGU

The tropical rain fell all night
Stopped just before the first cock crow
In slumber lay the village folk
While they slept the king made his round
Leaving his footprints as his hallmark
As the day broke, Undensi's goat was missing
Alarm raised, Hei! Obu agu O! Obu agu O!
Kill or be killed, was his only thought
Ignoring every plea not to go after the king.
Into the forest he went with his bow and arrows
Following the king's foot prints
Asleep after his heavy meal, he lay snoring
This chance he could not miss
His arrows rained like water on him
Leaving the king bleeding to death
The forest vibrated as he roared, roared and roared
The king of the forest lay dead
Far and near, the news spread
The greatest hero, he was cheered
Women danced and chanted his name
While the talking gong kept calling their hero
Udensi, now, became Ogbuagu by title.

UNCERTAINTY

The sun will rise and set
The moon and stars will shine at night
Night will fall and day will break
There will be dry and rainy seasons
Man will sow and man will reap
The cock will crow to tell the time
Crickets and frogs will be heard at night
My love for Africa will never die
The goat remains a vegetarian
Man will live and man will die
For me, will I be here tomorrow?

MAN'S ENEMY

Thou the king of wickedness
Mercilessly you continued
To claim your victims
Condemning them to prison cells
You've destroyed many a happy home
Many widows and orphans you have left
Unhealed many broken hearts
You brought the mighty to nothing
The weak you made weaker
Disaster and destruction are your rewards
Under your influence man has no control
Your slave he will continue to be
Until he learns to say No! No! No!
I have had enough.

THE IROKO TREES

Often I wondered
Where all the iroko trees have gone
Once they were the king of all the tropical trees
The best timber in the land
Although they take years to grow
When they do, immense wealth they give
To cut them, many rituals must be performed
This shows respect for the king of the trees
Was this too much I asked?
Why no one cared to defend their cause
Someone who could have stopped this terrible massacre
And prevent this terrible disaster.

VISITORS

Morning activities were over
Shortly after lunch
He sat quietly looking gloomy
What could be wrong, I said?
Often he would look at his watch
Then through the window and sigh
I then realised it was visiting time
"Hello," I said, "is everything all right?"
He forced a smile and replied
"Yes, yes, quite all right thank you."
Near the end of visiting time he became restless, his head low
As he looked up, his visitors were approaching
His face lit up like a Christmas tree
From then on, it was laughter all the way
I shook my head and said
"What a difference visitors make to patients."

YESTERDAY WAS MINE

As the night fades into day, the tropical rain ceased
Just as it began
Today is the big match
Sleepless night I had as I remembered yesterday
Once the captain of my team, twice nominated
best player of the year
I could hear them cheering my name
But today I cheer for them in my wheelchair
as I watch them perform
Ever so often I wish I could wind the clock back
Now I live in memories
Yesterday was mine I said
But today is theirs
Be thankful if you're amongst the players of today
Be thankful too if yesterday could bring you happy memories.

SPRING

Mmm ... the air is fresh, Spring is here
Although a bit chilly, this is expected
Frightened little beauties still asleep
The sun has come to wake you up.

The popping out of rose-buds and daffodils
Birds fill the air with their melody
As they hop from tree to tree
Telling us that Spring is here.

Soon, food will be plenty and easy to get
The migrated ones will soon return
Where are the hedgehogs? they should be here
Tell them that Spring is here.

Easter Festival falls in Spring
The singing of the Hallelujah Chorus
Nature soon to be crowned with unimaginable colours
Let there be Spring in every heart.

THEY FOUGHT FOR OUR FREEDOM

When we remember what they did
How and why they did it
No honour or praise should be too much to give
To people who fought for our freedom.

Some were too young, others in their prime
Leaving their loved ones behind
Knowing that they might never return
With courage they said their final goodbye.

Under rain and sun
They continued to march on
They had only one thing in mind
To fight until freedom was won.

When one fell, the other took his place
Knowing that the next bullet might be for him
As predicted he fell next victim
They suffered pain in silence.

Kill or be killed was what they faced
Some walked until their boots dropped off
Other died with theirs on
Day and night danger was staring at them.

They lay where they fell
We remember them as if it were yesterday
These were people who gave their lives
So that freedom would prevail.

LOSING SOMEONE SPECIAL

Losing someone special
Is the hardest time of all
And losing your son Ogechi
What can we say to ease your pain
He sent him here for a purpose.

When we remember your son
We remember the beauty of God's work
He let you have him for a while
Now He calls him home
He sent him here for a purpose.

We have no right to ask him why
He called him home early in the morning
As a father, He has every right
So we must be ready to let go
He sent him here for a purpose.

The joy he gave to his friends and family
Will never be forgotten
Trying to beat the time
His task he quickly completed
He sent him here for a purpose.

Although you loved him very dearly
His father in heaven loves him more
Let us thank God for sending him to us
We wish he could have stayed longer
He sent him here for a purpose.

My dear brothers and sisters
May you know that the sadness you are feeling
Is being felt by us too who knew him
We pray that his memories will continue to bring us joy
For he was sent here for a purpose.

CLOSER TO NATURE

Her wooden chair she took
Down to the spring with her niece she went
Looking for a quiet place to sit and dream
To watch nature display her beauty.

On a muddy ground she placed her chair
Watching the women as they washed cassava and clothes
Remembering she once did the same
Certain things have not changed she said.

Birds were flying from one bamboo tree to another
Providing her with sweet melody
Butterflies perched on cocoyam leaves
Admiring their colours, nature her artistry displayed.

Squirrels were busy picking palm-nuts
Unaware that someone was watching
Suddenly she gave a cough
Frightened they took to their heels.

The cool breeze made her eyes heavy
Although out there, there was scourging heat
She wished that time could stand still
This was the place she longed to be.

Surrounded by nature was her childhood
Little did she take note of them
Daily her love continued to grow
As she found herself closer to nature.

GIVE LOVE A CHANCE

Since you are gone life seems so empty
Nothing has ever been the same
Daily I roam like a sheep
In search of her master
Every night I cry myself to sleep
Remembering it was just a lover's quarrel
Give me another chance I pleaded
Take these chains off my hands
And stop this heart from breaking
Enemies we have become
Forgetting all the good times we had
I've grown, so have you
With love we'll surely make our dreams come through
One more chance is all I ask for
And let love do the rest.

MAN'S SKELETON

Every man has a skeleton in his wardrobe
Many of which he is afraid to face
No one else knows about them but him
Often he tries to forget they are there
On and off, they tend to pop out
His mind, like a haunted house has become
He hears voices and unexplained foot steps
His sleep turns into a nightmare
To escape he goes away
Like a shadow he is followed
Freedom will not be his until face to face they see
I too have a haunted house
Like a tortoise and his shell, I cannot escape them
Unless face to face we see
My sleep will turn into nightmare.

HAVEN'T GOT MUCH TIME HERE

Come home my son, come home
Won't you please come home?
He calls over the mountains
The green hills echoed His voice
While my Lord keeps calling me.

By the river side
Where the white lilies grow
The wind bears His gentle voice
My sins made me tremble
While my Lord keeps calling me.

My heart opened up
At the sound of His trumpet
Must get home before He calls again
For I haven't got much time here
While my Lord keeps calling me.

MONEY - THE BITCH

The bitch is wanted and loved by all
Nothing moves without her
I can only hope and pray
Never to let her be my boss
The bitch can save and kill
Turning friends into enemies
Once described as 'the root of all evils'
Has destroyed many a happy home
Man found her the greatest weapon
Which could destroy a nation
Not to be trusted as a friend
Here today, could be gone tomorrow
Difficult to get, easy to spend
I realise there is no true happiness in the bitch.

FALLING IN LOVE WITH NATURE

Like a bird in a cage
The love of nature has set me free
To fly to far away places
With strange sounding names.

Never realised how much the rising sun
Full moon at night, the sound of crickets
And the cock crow that tells the time
Have become part of my African childhood memories.

Once I fell in love with a tree opposite the bus stop
Many things I said to her
Could understand every word she said
I am not crazy, that I know.

Everything in the universe becomes alive
Nature becomes part of me
To love and be loved by them
Their mouths utter no deceits.

Day after day I fall in love
Yesterday, the palm trees and coconut trees
Today, the bank of Imo river
Who knows tomorrow, who will be next.

NEW YEAR CELEBRATION

Sitting on the veranda by her sister's side
Ngozi watched the moon rise behind the ube tree
Tomorrow will be New Year's Day and full moon too
There will be no leftover cooked foods
All pots washed and dried
There will be chanting and beating of drums at midnight
To welcome the New Year and send off the old
Early morning, the air was fresh, perfumed with flowers
Laughter could be heard all over the village
Joy filled the hearts of men
Soon, mothers' cooking will fill the air
Girls with ankle beads dancing from house to house
Families visiting one another
Looking forward to night-fall
When the moon will be full and shine brighter
Children will do the moon-dance
Some will listen to folk stories
Men drinking palm wine and talking politics
While mothers talk about their families and farms
It will be "goodnight," when the moon goes in.

JOURNEY INTO ETERNITY

It is the second day
And you still have not moved
You can neither hear nor see
Many visitors are here for you
Something is not right.

Your loved ones screaming uncontrollably
Friends searching for the right words to say
Some too shocked to utter words
Is there no way to ease their pain?
It seems you really do not care.

Please try to open your eyes and mouth
A word or two will do
Many have showered you with praises
Others playing your favourite tunes
Expecting you to join in.

You seem neither happy nor sad
Your bed looks rather odd to me
Do you feel comfortable? I wonder
Even nodding your head a little will do
I really don't know what else to say.

Who tied those hands of yours like that?
Your feet also bound
Like a prisoner in chains and handcuffs
Surely you are no criminal
Why did you not protest?

A white garment is all you have on
You, usually fond of colours
Are making little fuss over these things
Don't let them mess you up like this
You have always been my idol and hero.

Suddenly, I realised that this is it
You are no longer in control
It is His orders you must obey
Prepare for your journey home
The journey to eternity.

LONG AWAITED HOURS

Aware of dangers ahead
I was gripped with fear
My mouth opened and closed
Words have failed me
If only I could cry or scream to tell the world how I feel
Will they really listen or care that I asked?
Some will be minding their own business
Others might think me insane
Obiajuru my friend has gone for hours
Many things went through my mind
Suppose he did not make it?
Suppose the doctors say they were sorry?
Suddenly I spotted a nurse walking briskly
Watching her face, I asked, "will he be all right?"
"Yes, come and see," she said. "He is in recovery."
As I entered, I called his name
His eyes half opened, he muttered some words
With tears in my eyes, I kissed his pale lips
Sitting by his bedside, his hands I held tight
Reflecting, I watched in silence.

SCHOOL TIME

I was happy all day, darkness spoiled it
School starts tomorrow
Early morning calls
Not staying home with mother
To listen to my favourite stories.

The expected day, my anxiety increased
Night has gone too quickly
Mother was worried, my yam not eaten
As I grabbed my bag, off we went
Holding mother's hand was my only joy.

His first day she said to the teacher
Please take care of him,
Tears running down my cheeks
Afraid of what will happen next
With a kiss and smile, mother left.

Quiet and withdrawn
Too much on my mind
The teacher did her best
Yet nothing was right for me
So glad when mother picked me up.

My face beamed with a smile
She gave me a kiss and patted my head
Soon we were home
Rice and stew made my day
My eyes were heavy, I fell asleep, tomorrow is another day.

THE BOY NEXT DOOR

Wishing I could be like him
Never stopping to think
My blessings never counted
How I envied the boy next door.

His house next to mine
Beautiful garden full of roses
Pond in the middle, fishes of many colours
How I envied the boy next door.

His dad was tall and slim
Mother's face like Mona Lisa
Perfect was his life to me
How I envied the boy next door.

His dog as big as him
In a stable his horse was kept
Could one ask for more than this?
How I envied the boy next door.

"Hey" my friend through the garden he called
"Could I come in and play," he said
Delighted at once I agreed
How I envied the boy next door.

Down we sat, his story was sad
A lesson I've learnt from him
Contented, I prefer to be me
Never to envy the boy next door.

THE SEA OF PORTUGAL

There I sat motionlessly watching you
Never have I seen anything so beautiful
So clear I could see the sand below
To me, you are nature's masterpiece.

As I watched your waves come and go
Gently kissing the sand along the shores
With the blue skies above
You looked a matching pair.

Along your shores adorned with houses
Painted in white they stood in a row
Green mountains high above the waters
Looking down in admiration.

Ever so often the sea gulls took a dive
To wash themselves as clean as you
They love to walk along the sandy shores
That glitter in the sun.

They will never know
How much I envy them
I wish I could take a dive
Without the danger of drowning myself.

The sailors' boats are moving effortlessly
You were too calm for words
I could never have asked for a better sight
It is wonderful to be here.

Oh it's past eight already
Sad that I have to go
All good things must come to an end
Let me take this picture
Which will always remind me of you.

PUBERTY

Like the popping out of rosebuds and daffodils
In spring, they bloom, beautifully displayed
Nature, her breasts fully moulded
Attracting men like flowers attract bees
This is puberty, life is carefree.

Happy and contented, she feels
Fearlessly experiencing the joy of youth
Like spring flowers unafraid of frost
Bubbling with life, green as spring leaves
Like nightingales in the early spring, she sings.

Swinging her hips from side to side as she walks
Like green leaves swinging in the wind
Her song full of Hallelujah, the Easter chorus
As spring looks forward to summer
So she too looks forward to womanhood.

Sometimes dancing and hopping on the street
The ground like a cushion, she feels under her feet
Often passers-by take her to be crazy
Walking on her toes as she did
Not realizing how vulnerable youth can be.

This is an intoxicating stage of her life
For her one bullet cannot kill
Trying everything and daring nothing
Unprotected, will fade and fall like leaves before the summer
As she is unaware of dangers ahead.

CHRISTMAS

A chilly winter wind
Bringing snowflakes everywhere
Soon the snow begins to fall
Good news for one and all
Because it is Xmas day.

Everywhere looked immaculately white
As the snow continued to fall
Happy faces running around
Despite the cold, they continued to play
Because it is Xmas day.

Merry Xmas, Happy New Year
In the town and country too
There is excitement everywhere
As the Church bells continued to ring
Because it is Xmas day.

Time for caring, time for sharing
Goodwill and peace to everyone
Mothers cooking perfumes the air
Today we'll have turkey for dinner
Because it is Xmas day.

Although it is cold and biting
Causing the body to shiver
Still, warmth stays in our heart
Which burns with zeal and love
Because it is Xmas day.

FRIENDSHIP

Suddenly a vacuum is created
Accustomed warm feelings freeze
A cold wall stands like a barrier
Familiar voices sound hoarse and unfamiliar
We no longer recognize those we used to know.

Expressions freeze on their faces
They gaze and stare, speak strangeness
They speak and I listened in confusion
They move towards me and I shudder
What happened to the people we used to know?

Their behaviour kills expectations
Regrets set in and frightens
Conversations produce nightmares
Sharing accommodation deepens
Are these not those we once knew?

They talk in whispers
We are neither friends nor foes
It is difficult to categorize them
You watch unfamiliar eyes watching you
What happened to faces we used to know?

Do they see us the way we see them?
You move forward, they withdraw and speak in baffling tongues
They stand or sit and regard you as prey
Terrified, you shake under the unforeseen coldness
Are these people not those we used to know?

I AM A PERSON

Nurse, talk to me as a person please
Not as an old lady in bed number three
I have a name and status
Both of us are equal as human beings
The difference lies in our tasks
Yours to give, mine to receive; the carer and the patient.

I would love to be included
In every aspect of my treatment
After all, whose life is it?
Talk to me in layman's English
Medical terms frighten even the most intelligent
And these will add to my already loaded head.

Try to understand and be more sympathetic
A little caring and gentleness is all I ask for
Surely this is not too much to give
To somebody who was as anxious as myself
I know how busy you are trying to get things done
Remember today it is me, tomorrow it could be you.

Sometimes I might do something silly
Deep down I am afraid to admit
That losing control is hard to take
As I see it happening to me
Now I find myself helpless and in care
Surrender has never been one of my plans.

Remember that all day long I have nothing to do
By observations I can spot humanity and genuineness of heart
This is the quality of the nurse who makes me retain my dignity
She often goes unnoticed by colleagues
As she makes very little fuss
The smile on her face says it all.

When I mess myself as I often do
Although I might not say I am sorry
Deep down by my facial expression
You can see that I am sad and embarrassed
With my communication so poor
How can I put into words how I feel.

I really would like to know that you are my spokesperson
To remind the doctors of their bedside manners
It is you that I see more often
As a mother you know when and where I hurt
How I feel, sleep and my daily progress
You know because you care.

My relatives might become a nuisance to you
It is because they are anxious
Saying wrong things at the wrong time
It is not easy to watch your loved ones suffer
In time I hope that you will come to know them better
And say to yourself, they were not that bad after all.

I do not forget the fact that you are human
And as such have problems of your own
Your task can only be performed
By the dedicated ones like you
For no amount of money will pay for what you do
The joy and comfort you bring to people in pain
Will be remembered and treasured long after you have gone.

THE ABBEY WEPT

She never knew what to expect
Tomorrow everything will be clear
Although she had always been prepared
For the unexpected at all times.

This is one she has never seen before
And will never see for years to come
It seems that the nation is in mourning
And has come to a stand-still.

Standing there, many things went through my mind
Watching the mourners as they come in hundreds
It was the genuineness of their heart
That was difficult to believe.

For many people who were there
Every one came as an individual
Mourning her in their individual ways
Some with tears, others stood still in confusion.

Every age, race, creed and nationality
Describing her in their own words
As if they have knows her all their lives
The scene was breathtaking, mildly put.

The Abbey now accepts the fact
That the Princess will be here soon
This will also be her last visit
Like other mourners, she wept.

MY KIND OF LOVE

She must have been there all summer
Could one overlook such a beauty?
As I had done until tonight
Standing face to face with her.

Isn't she beautiful?
What is? asked a colleague standing by
Make sense, said she, angrily
For she could not see what I had seen.

Tired, aching legs waiting for the bus
Could think of nothing but getting home
Suddenly our eyes met with no words uttered
From then on my pains were forgotten.

Across the road we spoke to each other
In a language no one else could understand
Little did we know that we were falling in love
Nothing else mattered after that.

Day and night, dancing with the wind
Washed by rain, dried by the sun
Watching you come and go
Hoping that you could make time for a chat.

Often I cried when you passed me by
Always in a hurry, for duty calls
Tonight I was glad we finally met
Can't wait any more before I break.

Cold weather fast approaching
Soon will deprive me of my beauty
Come spring, in bloom I will be
Waiting like a bride for her groom.

Worry not my love, all is well
With or without your beauty
I will always love you.
When I fall in love, I stay in love.

Could I be losing my mind?
Can't remember anybody falling in love
With a tree amongst other trees.
My love, my queen, the tree opposite the bus stop.

THE OTHER SIDE

This is London, full of street lights
Where men and women come to seek their fortune
From every nationality, colour and creed
The very rich and the very poor
Magnificent tower buildings
Many places of interest
Some modern, others ancient
The Thames and her bridges
Underground and surface trains
Shopping centres to feed your eyes
Many places where money changes hands
People in fancy clothing and expensive cars
Everywhere you go you meet with bustling crowds
The rush hour is nothing to talk about
And many many more
It's a round-the-clock show
If you are tired of London, you are tired of life they say
But there is another London, silent as the dead of the night
I guess, London, you are not alone.

THE WANDERER

I love to wander by the stream that sparkles in the sun.
I love to wander along the mountains and valleys
Scenery often breathtaking.
I love to wander along the rustling waters as they make their
way through the rocks
Fishes of many colour swimming with ease.
I love to wander along the riverside where lilies grow
As the bees make their honey.
I love to wander through the bamboo trees, watching the birds
fly from tree to tree.
I love to wander by the coconut beach hoping that one will fall
but not on my head.
I love to wander in sunshine and in rain, to watch the waterfalls
come down the mountains.
I love to wander at dawn.
At sunset, I love to wander too
To laugh and sing beneath the clear blue sky.
I would love to wander until the day I die.

PLANTATION

Mothers little cocoa plantation
Grew down the stream in the valley where we live
Early morning until late evenings
Her time she spent pruning and weeding
Those little trees she treated like her children
Calling each one by its name
Although mother had many other farms
None gave her so much pleasure
As the little cocoa plantation down the stream where we live.

WAYWARD

Smiling and dancing on a coconut beach
Seducing men that came her way
She wants the best and paid the price
Soon she was alone with no one to care.

Watching the girl he used to know
Growing old before his eyes
His daughter once the beauty queen
Now dried up like the harmattan leaves.

Hips no longer swung from side to side
Starving face with sunken eyes
Like a leper she walked the street
Those she knew distanced themselves from her.

No pity left in the heart of men
Mercy, mercy she cried, with no one to hear
Her shadow was her only friend
Telling her the truth about herself.

Take me not like this she pleaded
As she fell people laughed and jeered
A child ran, closed her eyes, and prayed
Her guardian angel at last was there.

FEAR AND JOY

Weeping little Okeke sat watching helplessly
As his pet the goat lay motionless
Mouth frothing, soon she could be dead
"A few minutes ago she was all right," he said.

Mother rushed to the scene
Legs began to kick up in the air
Eyes rolling from side to side
While Okeke continued to sob.

"My pet, my friend, answer me,
Why did I let you out this morning?
Poisonous leaves you must have eaten
Now I stand to pay the price."

Palm oil poured in
As the goat's mouth was opened
An antidote for everything
Look, she is struggling to get up again.

"Maa, maa," cried the goat
Okeke leapt up in the air
Hugged mother and carried his goat
"Mother," he said, "you are a star."

DREAM

I was late coming home
The street dark and deserted
Strong and angry was the wind
Flying objects here and there.

No sign of life could be seen
A little dog running up and down
As if searching for his master
Sniffing the ground from time to time.

At a distance something approached
Difficult to describe, face unfamiliar
Spark of light emitting from the chest
Frozen with fear, I was unable to run.

Who is there? I asked, half choked
Legs trembling, teeth chattering
My house a few yards away from here.
Must continue, I said.

Up the dog ran, to walk beside me
I moved at a snail's speed, seized with fear
Now the figure has disappeared
Where could it be hiding, I asked.

Suddenly I woke up in a cold sweat
The clock on the wall struck four
I sighed with relief
Never happened, just a dream.

ON THEIR 25th WEDDING ANNIVERSARY

The day was like any other day
The couple weren't going to make a fuss
Just a quiet meal, and a walk in the park
Then home to recap on years gone by.

Life has not been easy
The usual ups and downs of marriage
Nothing was new about this
Somehow, this is their 25th Wedding Anniversary.

Everything suddenly changed
Their son came down the stairs
"Good morning and happy anniversary," said he
Three envelopes he handed to them.

"Open them accordingly," he said
"Be waiting and ready at six
To answer the gentleman's call."
Their smiles lit the room.

According to plan, everything went
As they answered the gentleman at the door
Across the road stood a convertible Rolls Royce
This and other things were theirs for the evening.

Neighbours watched in amazement
Simple working-class people, how could this happen to them
As the chauffeur drove off
Tears of joy ran down their cheeks.

If they live to be a hundred
What he did for them
Will be forever written in their hearts
Never to be wiped away.

THE GRAVEYARD AT DAWN

Early morning walking through the graveyard
Looking at the graves both new and old
Some with overgrown grass here and there
How much are we remembered after we have gone?

Such large areas of land
Inhabited by people who were
Once like you and I
I stood still, reflecting on what might have been.

Watching the diggers arranging flowers
Brought in different colours, shapes and sizes
Soon they too will wilt and die
Man has nothing here that lasts forever.

Ever so often the crows will fly past
Making sounds that they alone understand
Rose flowers giving off their perfume
Watered to keep their roots firm and alive.

The sun was hazy as it came through the clouds
The wind, gentle and cool, too
For some whose lives had been once a mad rush
Life here seems so quiet and peaceful
At last a resting place has been found.

Standing in front of the cemetery chapel
Tall trees in rows like columns of soldiers
Waiting for their general to take his final salute
Ready to direct him through to his final destination
For they know that life here is a mere stepping stone.

FRIENDSHIP II

Friendship blossoms
Like the summer rose
Cared for and watered
She grows, grows and grows.

Friendship blossoms
In good times and bad times
Always the same
She grows, grows and grows.

Friendship blossoms
Giving everything, accepting nothing
Living for one another
She grows, grows and grows.

Friendship blossoms
She never gets old
Friendship never dies
She grows, grows and grows.

TROPICAL RAIN

The air was hot, no cooling in sight
Land dry and grass parched
There is dust everywhere
Waiting for the tropical rain to fall.

As they walked, no shoes they wore
Heated sand, their feet were burnt
Man perspired salt and water
Waiting for the tropical rain to fall.

Bush fires here and there
Wildlife running for shelter
It's the survival of the fittest
Waiting for the tropical rain to fall.

Animal carcasses littered the land
Offensive odour filled the air
Rivers dry, fishes die
Waiting for the tropical rain to fall.

How much can man endure
Things we take for granted
Nature not fully appreciated
Waiting for the tropical rain to fall.

Rain maker! Rain maker!
Make rain not sun
Wait no more or else we'll die
Waiting for the tropical rain to fall.

TROPICAL RAIN II

Heavy wind, falling trees
The sky is heavy and black
Turning the day into night
Tropical rain belting down.

Rivers overflowing their banks
Water gushing down the mountains
Washing the soil as they go
Tropical rain belting down.

Everything is lush and green
The air fresh, ground breathes with ease
Wildlife flourishing everywhere
Tropical rain belting down.

There is joy in every heart
Man and beast alike
Birds sing, fishes swim
Tropical rain belting down.

The rain has gone
And all is clear
Soon they'll all forget
Before the rain, what happened

GRIEF MOTHER

The waiting was over
At last Ada was born
Mother's heart full of joy
The prettiest baby of all.

Curly hair, big brown eyes
Face like the African queen
Her smile like sunrays
Nature's masterpiece, she was.

Mama, the first word she spoke
At one, her first step she took
Mother thrilled with joy
Little did she know Ada was not here to stay.

Hot with fever, she was ill
Native doctor was called, news was bad
A phantom! the man declared
Too far gone, nothing could be done.

Mother, grabbed her baby and ran
Holding tight, she cried for help
Ada's body limp and cold
Gradually she closed her eyes.

"My baby, my love," mother screamed
Shattered with grief she cried aloud
Inconsolably, she cried and cried and cried
As her lifeless body lay in her arms.

DROUGHT

Come down, come down, oh please come down
Look what has happened to the plants
Some are dry and dying, the rest are dead
Oh won't you please come down.

Listen not to what men say
Men in search all the time
Never satisfied with what they have
Oh, won't you please come down.

Year after year you come and go
All the time taken for granted
Giving life to the land we live on
Oh won't you please come down.

The harmattan wind has done its worst
There is dust everywhere
Life has come to a standstill
Oh, won't you please come down.

Their thirst quenched when you arrived
The grass is green and life blossoms
Rivers overflow their banks
Thanks, at last, you've come.

THE PRISONER

Time ticks speedily on
Can't stop it ticking
It's ticking my life away
Yet it continues to tick.

"I'm mad driven by the tick," said Bongo
Twelve noon, soon it will be
Soon I will be gone
I wished I was never here.

Who will remember in a day or two
My passing as a prisoner
How quickly they'll all forget
Like a star, fading at dawn.

Hide me here, hide me there
But why was I so afraid?
This was destined to come
The price I have to pay.

With tears in my eyes, I pleaded
No one seemed to care
So many things I'd love to change
Sad, that I've got to go
Time! time! time! if only I had time.

FORGIVE AND FORGET

Forgive and forget, very often said
How easy could this be for me, I asked
Easier said than done, may be
Forgive, yes, forget could be difficult.

My mind is a marriage of two parts
Conscious groom with the subconscious bride
Controllable is the groom
Can store and retrieve information at will.

Bride, wild and uncontrollable
From time to time goes out of control
Revealing herself when I least expect
Memories exposed which cannot be erased.

Scars reopened which cannot be healed
Memories of my childhood based on remembering
Lasting me from youth to grey-hair days
Talking about good and bad times.

How difficult for me to forget
Now I know that I can forgive
But when I do remember the already forgiven
To forgive all over again and again
As many times as I remembered them.

AMBITION

Africa was Jack's greatest ambition
As danger she was portrayed
Determined, it's Africa or nothing
As he slept, dreams of doubts he had
Yet, he hoped and longed for Africa.

Thickened forest caused by torrential rain
Swampy land difficult to walk on
Tropical heat, that could melt steel
Her customs different from his
Yet, he hoped and longed for Africa.

Tribal wars determine the king
Initiated, or you don't belong
Colonies of man-eaters, roaming the land
Better be home, before night falls
Yet, he hoped and longed for Africa.

Expected day Jack finally sailed
At last, face to face with Africa he came
The truth was there for him to see
Treasures beyond his imagination
Beauty of the rising and setting sun.

The land of palms, and waterfalls
Mothers with babies on their backs
Girls with ankle beads, hair plaited
Children playing when the moon was full
The sound of crickets echoed every where.

Under the palm trees Jack sat
Delighted at last to be here
"No regrets, no regrets" he said
"Peace and contentment will fill my days
For here, nature has displayed her beauty."

LAMENTATION

Oh! how I remembered yester-years
As I walked bushy pathways
So many years have passed, so much has happened
Yet it seemed like yesterday
Every wound has a scar as its hallmark
Reminding us of the past.

Once life was good and carefree
We walked the streets without fear
Went wherever we wished, not minding the time
Slept in the open till the air was cool
Every spot, to children, was a playground
When night fell, every home was theirs.

Saturday night was special for both old and young
High-life music boomed from dusk till dawn
Love stirred the hearts of citizens
Brother cried and his brother heard
He was trusted, he spoke the truth
For then, his yes was yes, no was no.

The land was rich and fertile, the poor survived
Now dry, full of erosion she lies barren
Mighty Imo River spread from shore to shore
Fishes were plenty and easy to catch
Green grass all year round, now withering
The iroko trees were the king of all the trees
Like man, many have since been destroyed.

Years of progress has turned to years of destruction
Progress too, has turned brother against brother
Sister against sister, children against their parents
When will these dark clouds be lifted? I asked
As we drifted from bad to worse
And things continued to fall apart.

LOVED ONES NEVER DIE

When loved ones pass away
Inside feels so hollow
An emptiness nothing can fill
Their seats become vacant.

Life becomes a nightmare full of confusion
Darkness is all you can see
Tears flow uncontrollably
Sun has set at midday.

Black and grey clouds fill the sky
Friends try to help the best way they know
Some unable to find the right words
But comforting in their own little way.

Their presence make a lot of difference
These are the friends indeed
For, left alone, you sink beneath the waves
In time, nature continues to heal her wounds.

Gradually, the black clouds lift
Letting the sun shine through
Memories are all that is left
And an appreciation you were never alone.

THE LOVERS

On the bank of the Eru river
There Ebere stood waiting for Obi
We'll meet at sunrise he promised
She waited, he was nowhere in sight.

Tropical sun at noon, unbearable it becomes
Shelter, she was forced to seek
Coconut tree, natures shade provider
She waited, he was nowhere in sight.

Sincere, my love, he has been
Trusted, have no cause to doubt
Tears rolled, unable to control
She waited, he was nowhere in sight.

Frustrated and weary, she began to walk
Immaculate white, lilies she admired
Nature so beautiful, so should man be, she said
She waited, he was nowhere in sight.

By the river bank, she has fallen
The air was cool, birds singing melodies
Her eyes heavy, sleep soon to follow
She waited, he was nowhere in sight.

As she woke watching the sunset
Her eyes were full of tears
Knowing that he will never be there
Broken-hearted, she walked slowly home.

LUCKY AND ME

Lucky, my dog was lucky
Never has a boy been so happy as me
I was lucky and so was he
It was luck that brought us together.

Thrown on the street and left to die
Roamed the land in search of love
Found by father who brought him home
It was luck that brought us together.

Collar was tight, around his neck
'Not wanted,' read his tag
Too old to live, no longer can perform
It was luck that brought us together.

Tired and hungry unable to bark
Kindness and love put him on the mend
Spoilt by all, Lucky was happy
It was luck that brought us together.

If I live to be hundred
Never will I have another pet like Lucky
We were inseparable, mother commented
It was luck that brought us together.

For pets who were not so lucky as Lucky
Help might come too late or never
They might not be lucky as Lucky
It was luck that brought us together.

SILVER WEDDING ANNIVERSARY

To: Ruth and Joshua
Silver Wedding Anniversary
25 years of togetherness
Being there for each other
Walking the rough and smooth roads
Loving, caring, and supporting
In bad times and good times
Being the best of friends
Trusting and believing in one another
Listening and hearing what was said
Accepting each other the way you are
Children as they arrived
Re-arranging your lives from A-Z
Pains and joys they brought
Yet, your marriage vows you tightly gripped
On reflection, you whispered
"If I had to choose again,"
"I would always choose you.

A NURSE AND MY IDOL

If I visited the sick with my mother
I would touch a nurse smiling
She would take me round the ward
Like a diminutive nurse, I tarried.

Sitting with mother, I watched her attend to the patients
She walked quietly and briskly
Her uniform was immaculately white
Her shoes, polished and shiny.

She spoke with soft and gentle voice
The smile on her face beamed like sunlight
Comforting and reassuring were her words
She seemed respected by those she cared for.

Suddenly crisis erupted, call-bell ringing continuously
Quickly she came with a pan
After which, the air was never the same
Yet her facial expression remained unchanged.

As mother and I were leaving
I hugged and kissed my idol nurse
"You are my role model," I said
With a smile, "Thank you," she replied.

All night I dreamt of my idol nurse
Whose smile beamed and lit the ward
How I wish I could emulate my idol nurse
To walk, talk and care just like her.

THE PALM TREES

Walking along your path
The air was fresh and cool
You stood like soldiers on guard
Others scattered here and there.

When the wind blows
Your leaves seem to sing melodies
Sweet to send a man to sleep
My beautiful palm trees.

You are the sanctuary
Of creatures great and small
Your leaves for birds to build their nests
Squirrels there to pick your nuts.

From you, many a man his wealth has made
So much you give to us
Nothing from you is wasted
The land where you grew is blessed.

I could watch you endlessly
Is there any chance we could speak?
So much I would like to tell you
To confess the magnitude of my love
With you my secret is safe.

DISAPPOINTMENT

Loving you is all I ever wanted
You are the source of my happiness
Devoted to you with all my heart
Darling, how could you forget so soon?

Remember all the love letters you wrote
Promises you vowed never to break
Not once did any doubts cross my mind
Darling, how could you forget so soon?

Over the years our plans continued
Too young to marry, mother often said
But our love was too strong to break
Darling, how could you forget so soon?

At last, our wedding day in May was set
Can't wait for the wedding bells to ring
Hand in hand by your side to walk
Darling, how could you forget so soon?

May has come and gone
It is now the month of June
Yet no sound of our wedding bells ringing
Darling, how could you forget so soon?

Someone has taken my place, I know
Forgetting you will not be easy
But I'll get along somehow
Darling, how could you forget so soon?

UDEZE AND THE LAW

The cry of the village night watchman
Telling it was past midnight
He quickened his step, his heart beating like a drum
No one should be seen on the street at this time.

Will they understand if he tries to explain?
He was amongst the law makers
No one is above the law, he said
Even I, Udeze, is no exception.

Gangs of robbers terrorised the village
Streets were unsafe at night
People feared for their lives
That's why the law was brought into force.

As he turned his key he was gripped by fear
A tap he felt on his shoulder
His legs became weak and shaky
He disappeared and was never seen again.